T0087875

WORLD'S FAVORITE

MOZART BEST KNOWN PIANO SONATAS

COMPILED BY

ALEXANDER SHEALY

FOREWORD

Except for the Sonata in C Minor, from which we are including only the "allegro" movement, the 13 Sonatas in this volume are presented in their entirety.

The Sonatas are reproduced in their original (urtext) form, from original Mozart manuscripts, first editions and earliest available copies autographed by the master.

Since all have been originally entitled simply "Sonata", we are distinguishing and identifying them by the keys in which they were written. All of the Sonatas were written in at least two keys.

We consider this volume as a most important and essential adjunct to the library of anyone who appreciates the greatness of the composer and his music.

The Publisher

WOLFGANG AMADEUS MOZART

(Pronounced Mote-zart)

Born Salzburg, Austria, January 27, 1756
Died Vienna, Austria, December 15, 1792

Wolfgang Amadeus Mozart was the son of Leopold Mozart, an accomplished musician (violinist, composer and chapel master at the court of the Archbishop of Salzburg). Wolfgang showed promise as an infant and composed little pieces when he was only four. His father gave music lessons both to Wolfgang and to his somewhat older sister, Marianne. When he was only six years old, his father decided to take him and his sister on concert tours. The boy's genius aroused great enthusiasm. By the time he was 16, he took part in concerts in leading European cities.

When in Italy, he was inspired to compose (later in Vienna) three operas which were destined for world wide acclaim, Don Giovanni, The Marriage of Figaro and The Magic Flute.

Mozart was married in 1782 to Constance Weber of Munich. They had six children, but only two survived his own premature death.

In spite of ill health and poverty (having been cheated out of his profits from his successful operatic works), he composed over 600 works in his short life span. He goes into history as one of the world's greatest composers of all time. Outstanding among his masterpieces are the Requiem (commissioned by one Count Walseck in memory of his dead wife), a dozen great symphonies, fifteen brilliant piano concertos, music for string quintets, sonatas, sonatinas, rondos and minuets.

All of Mozart's works reveal perfection in craftsmanship and a seemingly endless flow of creative melody in a great variety of moods.

GENERAL COMMENTS

200 years have elapsed since Mozart's sonatas began their career toward their destiny of seemingly eternal life. Many debates have centered around them. Some musicologists point out their inferiority to the Beethoven sonatas, some attest to their superiority! Which of the Mozart sonatas are generally considered the greatest? In my humble opinion, each and all are worthy of the composer of the "Jupiter Symphony" and the "Magic Flute". The most popular have been the Sonata in A (from which the "Alla Turca" movement has individually made its way into every corner of the world) and the Sonata in C-G (its melodious theme having spread throughout the world of popular music).

Mozart's sonatas have been referred to as "the reanimation of classic art and literature" or as "models of graciousness and sweet reasonableness". We do not find the massive effects, the sonorous majesty and the grand design of the pianoforte sonatas of Mozart's successor, Ludwig van Beethoven, but we do recognize shapeliness of melody, pure transparency of texture and elegant finish of style.

Mozart was especially ingenious in altering the shape of his figures, changing the same theme from one hand to the other and introducing various original devices, so that there is no chance of monotony. He exhibits superb skill in contrapuntal treatment, adorning his work with ingenuities, without overloading the delicate texture of the music. Schubert may rival him as a creator of melody, Beethoven in massive construction of imperishable monuments, Haydn in broad style, force and pungency, but Mozart stands unrivalled in the delicacy of decorative sense, the building of a multitude of fragile materials which prove to be no less enduring throughout the centuries!

ALEXANDER SHEALY

MOZART SONATAS

CONTENTS

THEMATIC INDEX

SONATA
(C-G)

WOLFGANG AMADEUS MOZART

9

Andante

RONDO

SONATA
(Am-F-A)

WOLFGANG AMADEUS MOZART

Allegro maestoso

19

Andante cantabile con espressione

28

31

SONATA
(C-F No. 1)

WOLFGANG AMADEUS MOZART

SONATA
(C-F No. 2)

WOLFGANG AMADEUS MOZART

Allegro con spirito

RONDEAU

Allegretto grazioso

61

64

SONATA
(F-Fm)

WOLFGANG AMADEUS MOZART

Allegro assai

71

74

SONATA
(F-Bb No. 1)

WOLFGANG AMADEUS MOZART

Allegro

According to the manuscript:

According to the original edition:

Allegro assai

SONATA
(F-Bb No. 2)

WOLFGANG AMADEUS MOZART

Allegro

RONDO
Allegretto

117

SONATA
(Bb-Eb)

WOLFGANG AMADEUS MOZART

Adagio

Allegretto

SONATA
(G-C)

WOLFGANG AMADEUS MOZART

Allegro

131

135

Presto

139

SONATA
(C Minor)
Allegro Movement

WOLFGANG AMADEUS MOZART

Allegro

SONATA
(D-A)

WOLFGANG AMADEUS MOZART

Allegro

Adagio

157

159

164

SONATA
(Eb-Bb)

WOLFGANG AMADEUS MOZART

Adagio

MENUETTO I

MENUETTO II

Men. I D. C.

Allegro

SONATA
(A-D-Ab)

WOLFGANG AMADEUS MOZART

Andante grazioso

175

VARIATION I

VARIATION II

VARIATION III

VARIATION IV

VARIATION V
Adagio

VARIATION VI

Allegro

184

TRIO

(Menuetto D.C.)

ALLA TURCA
Allegretto

189